What This Book Will Do for You

By the time you finish reading this book, you will be able to decide for yourself if you are a good coach, and you will have learned how to make the coaching process work for you, how to set goals and standards, how to diagnose actions for change, and how to coach and counsel effectively.

Other Titles in the Successful Office Skills Series

COACHING
and
COUNSELING
in the
WORKPLACE

Donald H. Weiss

amacom

American Management Association

New York • Atlanta • Boston • Chicago • Kansas City • San Francisco • Washington, D.C.
Brussels • Toronto • Mexico City

This publication is designed to provide accurate and authoritative
information in regard to the subject matter covered. It is sold with
the understanding that the publisher is not engaged in rendering
legal, accounting, or other professional service. If legal advice or
other expert assistance is required, the services of a competent professional person should be sought.

Library of Congress Cataloging-in-Publication Data

Weiss, Donald H., 1936–
    Coaching and counseling in the workplace / Donald H. Weiss.
        p.   cm. — (The successful office skills series)
    Includes bibliographical references and index.
    ISBN 0-8144-7818-2
    1. Employees—Counseling of.   2. Personnel management.
I. Title.   II. Series.
HF5549.5.C8W45   1993
658.3'85—dc20   93-10602
                                                        CIP

Printing number

10   9   8   7   6   5   4   3

CONTENTS

Conventional wisdom maintains that 80 percent of a group's productivity comes from 20 percent of its people. If this is true, it means we're wasting 80 perent of our payroll on nonproductive or relatively nonproductive employees; we might as well fire that mass of costly people. But then we'd be left with only 20 percent of the people we need, and 80 percent of them wouldn't be productive enough to make them worthwhile, and we'd have to fire them, too. Soon, only one person would be left to do all the work. Doesn't make sense, does it?

Maybe that's because the conventional wisdom is wrong. Supervisors probably get more productivity from people than they know; most supervisors don't keep the kind of records they need for determining who is productive and who is not, anyway. On the other hand, you usually know when someone needs help or guidance or when someone is violating company rules and needs direction. That's where coaching and counseling come in: coaching helps people take action to improve their performance or to grow professionally, and counseling helps them bring their behavior into line with company policies and procedures. The processes of coaching and counseling are similar; when we talk about one, we are really talking about the other at the same time. In fact, at times we use the convention "coach/counselor" to reflect their similarities.

This book will show you ways to do both. We'll help you understand what a good coach does, talk you through ways of diagnosing problems, and end with steps for helping others improve their performance or grow professionally and change their behavior (counseling). Along the way, we'll talk about how to encourage other people and how to reinforce the positive results you're looking for.

CHAPTER ONE

Are You a Good Coach?

What is a good coach? That's a bit hard to define, but we can easily describe what a good coach does.

When I lead executive development programs, we do an exercise in which half the group volunteers to go to dinner blindfolded while the ''sighted'' participants act as their guides and coaches. We lead the blindfolded volunteers through the hotel's hallways, go outside (weather permitting), and head through the lobby and up or down the stairs before entering the dining room, where the volunteers eat dinner, still wearing their blindfolds. After returning to the main meeting room, we ask them to talk about their experiences, especially about their feelings and what they liked or didn't like about the way they were coached. Here are some representative answers.

"At first, I felt scared, helpless, but then, when [my coach] said, 'I'll help you,' I felt better, more secure."

"I felt dependent, out of control. I don't like not being in control. First, I felt angry about being dependent on [my coach], but when she took my elbow and steered me to where I had to go, I felt better, more in control than I thought I could be without eyes."

"[My coach] let me do things for myself. He set up an action plan. Told me where I had to go while we were walking without pushing me. Described the layout of the table—like a clock—the top of the plate 12 o'clock, water to my right at 2 o'clock—that sort of stuff. Then, when the food came, he let me cut up my salad and eat it by myself. He didn't treat me like a baby the way I expected he would."

"I felt really frightened at first. I've never done anything like this before, and I thought I'd make a fool of myself. Then, I got angry because [my coach] didn't give me much help. If I hadn't heard [another coach] tell her person how many steps there were, I think I would have fallen down. So I told [my coach], please tell me what to expect, and I think I can navigate pretty well on my own. I did, too. Well, at least I didn't stick my fork up my nose or spill my coffee in my lap."

"[My coach] really helped me a lot. He was very caring but didn't do everything for me. He just saw to it that I did everything I had to do. As we walked, I became more confident, but when I bumped into the door frame on the way into the dining room, I became angry with [my coach] until I realized he did tell me that the door frame was on my right; I didn't realize how close to my side it was. I should have asked more questions when I didn't understand or wasn't sure of what he meant. He apologized and made sure his instructions were clear throughout dinner.''

What's emerging are the characteristics of an effective coach, the nature of the relationship between the coach and the coachee, and the steps needed for effective coaching and counseling. Now, connect all this to your own experience by thinking back to a time when you needed help to improve your work or give your career a boost. Think about a time in your life when someone— a supervisor, a teacher, a coach, a coworker, or a teammate—came forward and helped you find a better way of doing something or a new path to follow.

What made your coaching experiences successful for you? What did the coach you appreciated the most do? What about her made you feel good about her? In short, what characterizes the excellent coaches or counselors you have known? Write down a list of their outstanding characteristics. (If you can't find someone in your personal experience, make a list of the people whom you admire for their ability to get the best from other people and list the characteristics that you admire.) Once you've finished, restart your reading at this point.

Characteristics of an Effective Coach/Counselor

If you're like most people, you recalled a person who cared about you, cared about how you performed. That person knew what had to be done and believed that you were capable of doing it and doing it well. He also knew enough about what you were doing to provide adequate guidance, even though he might not have been able to do it expertly. Have you ever seen Olympic gymnastic team coaches do the flips they teach those little children to do?

The coach we'll be looking at throughout this book is Katie Gardenia, a fictitious person based on many real people who have been successful coaches. Her work illustrates the principles of effective coaching and counseling. Katie is the supervisor of a graphic arts department in an advertising firm and has the challenge of helping Melissa Brand, a bright and talented artist, make the adjustment from school to her first professional job. This is no easy task, but Katie shows us how an effective coach and counselor rises to the occasion.

Katie: I'm turning this project over to you. I think you can handle it, and, of course, I'm always available if you need me.

Melissa: Are you sure I'm ready for this? This account's pretty important.

Katie: You'll do just fine. Everything you've done so far has worked well.

Melissa: Yes, but I've always been a member of a team. I've never soloed before.

Katie: Think of it as a class project. You soloed on those, and you aced them all.

Melissa [*still not sure*]: What if I bomb?

Katie: You won't, but if you do, I'll take my lumps, too. But I have confidence in you to do a superior job, and that'll make me look good, too. Now, I've shown you the first steps I would take. You take it from there. You have a week to get me preliminary drawings. That should be plenty of time, and I'll check in with you periodically to see if I can help. Don't fret so much; you'll produce your own creative blocks that way.

The following list includes all the characteristics of a good coach/counselor that we've illustrated in that dialogue.

A Good Coach/Counselor Is:

- A positive Pygmalion
- Enthusiastic
- Caring
- Supportive, trusting
- Focused, goal-oriented
- Knowledgeable
- Attentive
- Clear and concise
- Patient
- Observing, responsive

Positive Pygmalion: Katie's what we call a positive Pygmalion. She believes in her protegé and encourages her to do her very best. Studies show that a coach's attitude toward the people he coaches plays an important role in their performance. If you think the coachees can't do it, the chances are they won't do it or won't do it well. If you believe the contrary, they will come to believe it as well. Self-fulfilling prophecies work for good or for ill.

Enthusiasm: Positive Pygmalions reinforce both good feelings and positive results. Their enthusiasm is infectious. And, why shouldn't a coach feel good about the person she has picked to do the job? Enlightened coaches recognize that, if the other person does well, that success reflects well on them.

Caring: You have to care, as Katie does, about the welfare of the other person. Caring shows both in what you say or do and in how you say it or do it. Sincerity and respect are cornerstones in the coaching process.

Support and Trust: Without caring, you can't provide the support your coachees need. Your support—both moral and actual—assists the other person when necessary and creates trust. Let a blindfolded person walk into a wall and see how quickly she'll lose faith in you and in what you say or do.

Focus, Goal Orientation: Knowing what has to be done, by when, and by whom helps the people you're coaching to focus on results. You have to set expectations that are high enough to stretch people's skills but that are not out of reach. Katie sets goals and objectives for herself as well as for Melissa. She gave Melissa one week to complete her preliminary drawings. That is, she told Melissa what she expected and when she expected it.

Knowledge: You can't fake knowledge when you're coaching someone. "I don't know, but we can find out" is the best response to a question you can't answer. Likewise, you don't have to do what it is you're telling someone else to do. Encouraging someone to go back to school in order to grow and to enhance her opportunity to advance doesn't require that you go back to school yourself, but you have to know that going to school will be helpful. If you're showing someone how to improve on the quality of his work, you should know what standards or results will do the job.

Attentiveness: To be a good coach, you have to listen well, clear your desk as well as your mind, focus on what the other person is saying, and listen actively by making comments or asking questions for clarification. Active listening encourages other people to open up to you when they need a sounding board or help. That way they *give* you opportunities to coach or counsel them.

Clarity and Conciseness: You have to give instructions that the other person can follow and understand with a minimum of effort for your coaching to have value or effect.

Patience: Even though Katie knows what has to be done, she understands that changing behavior or learning new skills takes time. So she pointed Melissa in the right direction, rather than telling her exactly what to do. Patience is very important.

When you coach someone, you must be conscious of the *learning curve.* Katie, at the top of the curve, is *unconsciously competent.* She doesn't have to think about what comes next. She just does it. On the other hand, Melissa, at the bottom of the curve, is *unconsciously incompetent.* At this stage of her development, she doesn't know what it is she doesn't know. Katie points out to her the next step she has to take and so starts her up the learning curve; now Melissa is *consciously incompetent,* but she's ready to learn. At the next stage of development, Melissa will become *consciously competent.*

It's now the next day.

Katie: Hi, Melissa. How's it going?

Melissa: I'm struggling with it. Here's a first sketch related to the top of the line.

Katie: Hmm. I'm afraid I'm struggling with it, too.

Melissa [*a bit discouraged*]: I think I need to come up with a fresh approach.

Katie: Have you reviewed the slogans the wordsmiths generated?

Melissa: I was just getting them out of the file when you came in.

Katie: Good. Well, I've a meeting with my boss. We'll probably be at it until late. So I'll see you in the morning. Good start, Melissa. Keep it up.

Observation and Responsiveness: While your employee is becoming consciously competent and is on her way to becoming unconsciously competent, you have to be aware of what she is doing and how well she is doing. A good coach has to see and understand what the other person needs in order to help the person improve or grow. You have to become observant and responsive to what you observe.

Being responsive means giving both positive and negative feedback. Feedback doesn't mean criticism. It doesn't even mean that oxymoron— ''constructive criticism.'' It means, in this context, telling someone what you like and don't like, what affects you positively and what affects you negatively. It's information that the other person can use to make a change in his or her performance or behavior. Positive feedback supports doing something well or doing something right. Negative feedback makes a request for change.

After Katie goes to her meeting, Melissa leaves work early, without telling anyone. And she doesn't read the slogans they discussed. Here's what Katie does the next day.

Katie: My meeting ended early. When I walked by your drawing board, I realized you were gone.

Melissa: I left early.

Katie: No one knew you were leaving early.

Melissa: I guess not.

Katie: You know we don't keep people on a leash here, but we do need to keep up with everyone, and we do ask that you tell at least our secretary that you're going for the day. And we also ask that you tell me your plans.

Melissa: It was just an impulse. I felt all bottled up and needed to get out—walk it off.

Katie: It's just this one time, so it's no big deal, but in the future, please let me know what you want to do or leave me a note if I'm tied up. It's a question of perception, Melissa.

Melissa: I don't understand.

Katie: People have to perceive that you're dependable—that you're here when you're supposed to be and that they can rely on you if they need you.

Melissa: That makes sense.

Katie: Let's get back to work. We'll chalk up this one as a learning experience.

Whether you're coaching or counseling, to be effective, you have to be focused and goal-oriented—or, to put it another way, firmly resolved.

If you ever saw the film *My Fair Lady*, you'll remember that Henry Higgins had plenty of firm resolve, but he lacked patience, caring, and genuine attentiveness—that is, until Eliza Doolittle taught him how important they are. Only then did he become a good coach to whom his coachee could respond in kind.

CHAPTER TWO

How to Make the Coaching Process Work for You

❦

By now you've surmised that coaching or counseling is not an event that happens all at one time. Coaching benefits both the coach and the person being coached only if it's an ongoing process that has to be nurtured—not only by the coach but by the coachee as well—to make it work.

Benefits of Coaching and Counseling

Just think about the 80 percent of our staff that the conventional wisdom would have us fire.

What a waste. No one benefits from creating that much upheaval—especially not the people in that 80 percent.

Some people are mismatched with their jobs or are incapable of learning or of becoming blazing stars in their professions, and some people just can't seem to conform to company policies and procedures. Still, it's unhealthy to devote all your attention to only the stars. Give stars their recognition and reinforcement, but give the masses of hard workers your attention, as well. Coaching and counseling benefits everyone: the individual, the coach or counselor, and the organization as a whole.

Benefit to the Coachee: Individuals benefit from coaching by doing better than they did before or by growing or developing. Coachees may be late bloomers who, through careful nurturing, can become the stars that only you believe they can become. Many people owe their success to one person who had a great amount of faith in them.

Benefit to the Coach: The coach benefits by earning the coworker's or employee's loyalty. Usually, people you help will go out of their way to help you in turn. (Yes, there are those rotten scoundrels who'll use you and turn on you the first chance they get. Novels and movies about them are interesting because such people are the exceptions, not the rule.) Additionally, you feel good when someone you help succeeds. In most business environments, people who help other people develop receive recognition through rewards, compensation, and promotion. You get ahead by helping others get ahead.

Benefit to the Organization: The organization benefits by having more productive, more loyal, and more enthusiastic employees. Coaching and counseling are bottom-line activities that reduce the incidence of costly turnover, absenteeism, slowdowns, and accidents.

Characteristics of the Coaching/ Counseling Process

The coaching process, like a good coach, has recognizable characteristics that you can recreate.

Mutual Support: The coaching process must be characterized by a mutual respect between you and the other person and a belief in each other and in what each of you brings to the process. Remember the remarks from one of the blindfolded people's experience? She needed to find things out for herself and also needed to feel that the coach was there to guide her and to provide the information she needed to succeed. The blindfolded volunteer's coach, on the other hand, respected her abilities as well as her "disabilities."

Characteristics of the Coaching/ Counseling Process

- Mutually supportive, characterized by mutual respect
- Productive, creating an environment conducive to learning, to making mistakes and learning from them
- Trusting, fostering a nonpunitive atmosphere in which openness and candor exist

---

He also respected her adulthood. Being blind-folded didn't make her stupid or take away past experience that she could use to orient herself to her new circumstances.

At the same time, the blindfolded volunteer respected her coach's need for information and feedback from her. He couldn't know what she understood or didn't understand unless she told him. For the coach to be able to help, the coachee had to participate in the coaching process, not just passively receive it.

The more both you and the coachee contribute to the coaching process, the deeper your respect for one another will grow. Questions such as "What do you think you might do here?" or "How do you think you should approach the situation?" or "What do you think you need from me?" will help you orient yourself to what the coachee requires. They will also signal to that person your expectation that she will participate in her own learning and that you have confidence in her.

Productive Environment: Mutual respect creates a productive environment, one that is conducive to learning (and without a productive environment, mutual respect cannot flourish). We don't mean merely the physical surroundings; the greatest amount of learning can go on in the shabbiest of places (which happens in inner-city schools all the time). We're talking about an environment in which the learner can make mistakes and learn from them without fear of dire punishment.

An excellent example of this occurred in Chapter 1, when Melissa left early without telling anyone. Katie could have come down on her, but she didn't. Melissa made a false start on her art-work, as well, but instead of criticizing her or telling her exactly what to do, Katie suggested that the young artist do some more research.

Trust: Without trust, nothing can happen. We're repeating ourselves deliberately because nothing is more important than trust in the coaching relationship.

A punitive atmosphere breeds fear, and fear destroys trust; where fear and distrust exist, openness and candor can't exist. On the other hand, mutual respect induces trust. Here's an illustrative conversation between Katie and Melissa.

Katie: Reread the campaign material. Give the drawing another shot. I think you'll find new ideas every time you read what the writers want to communicate.

Melissa: You've done campaigns like these so many times before, I can't see why you want me to do this. You'd do in two days what'll take me two weeks.

Katie [*smiling*]: Probably, but before I could, I had to learn how. It would have taken me two weeks when I first started. I think you can do a good job of it, and it'll mean a lot to you if you work at it. All I can do is quote Thomas Edison — success is 10 percent inspiration and 90 percent perspiration.

Melissa [*gathering up her note pad; at the door*]: I believe you know what you're doing, but you've more faith in me than I have in myself.

Trust, openness, and candor — if you're going to be a successful coach and counselor, you'll have to develop all of these. But it's not something you can do alone.

Characteristics of the Person Being Coached or Counseled

You have probably noticed that Katie can't take all the credit for her successful relationship with Melissa; Melissa gets a lot of the credit, too. Many mentoring programs fail because the people chosen to be mentored don't want it. This has been the sad experience in many school drug abuse prevention programs. The youngsters feel as if they're targets, rather than partners in the relationship.

Melissa exhibits all the characteristics of an effective coachee.

Openness: Melissa's a willing partner. She's nervous about "soloing," but she's open to new ex-

---

Characteristics of a Successful Coachee

- Open to new experiences, willing to do something new or different
- Responsive, willing to listen to other people, to accept negative as well as positive feedback, to take instructions, and to do what is expected
- Assertive, willing to ask for help, clarification, or additional instruction or guidance
- Goal-oriented, focused on producing results or changes
- Enthusiastic, eager to learn

---

periences and willing to do something new or different. You can encourage openness by preparing the other person for the new experience—for example, letting him watch you do something you want him to do or asking her to read something on a new subject or procedure. You can also encourage openness by letting your coachee know that you believe that she can do what you (or someone else) are doing.

Responsiveness: Melissa's responsive, willing to listen to her supervisor. She's willing to take feedback, to take instructions, and to do what is expected. This, too, is behavior you have to encourage.

You may have noticed that we keep using the word *feedback*, rather than *criticism*. Criticism is destructive. When you criticize, you imply that you know or can do everything, that you're always right. Feedback, on the other hand, gives support and guidance at the same time: "I like what you did here, Melissa, but there—something seems missing—a bold color or perhaps another figure. What do you think?"

Assertiveness: Melissa is assertive. She's willing to ask for help, for clarification, or for additional instruction or guidance. She's willing to stand up for what she thinks is right, but not offensively— "I think another figure would clutter up the foreground—detract from the center."

Again, you have to encourage the other person to be assertive. If Katie comes down on her here, too, she'll close the channels of communication between them.

Katie: You may be right. Still, I don't find the foreground jumping out at me enough, and that's where your message is.

Melissa: I'll play with it and bring it back later.

Focus, Goal Orientation: Like Katie, Melissa's goal-oriented. She's focused on producing results, and she's willing to make changes in order to get them. She knows that the goal of her drawing isn't to please herself, but rather to sell a product. She'll do whatever it takes to achieve that goal. You encourage that type of focus by reinforcing positive results and by rewarding the person for success.

Enthusiasm: Not only do you have to be enthusiastic about working with the person you're coaching, but that person also has to be enthusiastic about working with you and about working on your project together. When a person comes to you with a problem or with a question about the future, the enthusiasm is built in. On the other hand, when you have to bring a problem to the other person, you need to encourage enthusiasm by pointing out the benefits to him if he takes steps to solve the problem. Most people will be enthusiastic, eager, and committed to a change if they see what's in it for them if they make the effort.

In short, the person being coached ideally mirrors the coach's traits in many ways. If a perfect match doesn't exist, the situation is made more difficult, but it's not impossible.* It's worth everyone's while to make an effort with employees who show promise, although they are not per-

---

*For detailed discussions of the less than ideal situations, see two other titles in the SOS series: *How to Deal With Difficult People* and *How to Get the Best Out of Other People.*

forming up to standard or are violating company rules.

CHAPTER THREE

How to Set Goals and Standards

You can't get from here to there unless you know where there is. That aphorism, borrowed from Lewis Carroll's *Alice in Wonderland*, defines the process of setting goals and standards when coaching or counseling people. To get what you want from other people, both you and they need to know what you expect from them. Whether you're using counseling to take corrective action to change behavior or coaching to guide a person to a higher level of achievement, you need to create a context that directs the employee to a desirable result.

Business Goals

In an office setting, regardless of your personal goals, you have to be concerned about business goals. If you're the supervisor, it's your responsibility to guide people toward those goals.

Business goals fall into one of four categories:

1. Profits
2. Leadership (market share)
3. Development (new products)
4. Growth (increasing company size)

Unless a business achieves those goals, it's likely to stagnate and die.

You need to know which of those goals is or are currently of greatest concern to your company, because the company may change its goal, depending on business conditions. You can't just assume that the desire for *immediate* profits is behind everything the company does. To increase market share (leadership), the company may have to reduce profits by spending more on advertising. To develop new products, the company may have to invest in research and development and in training or retraining its labor force, again reducing profits. Increasing the company's size takes capital and also reduces profits. Any one of the four goals can command the company's agenda—at least for the time being.

Melissa: Katie, I'm afraid of letting you down.
Katie: What's the problem?
Melissa: I'm not moving as quickly on that project as I'd like. The longer I take to do it, the higher the cost and the longer it'll be before we get paid.
Katie: That's all true, but what's most important about this account?
Melissa: It'll open the door to a lot of similar accounts.
Katie: We'd really grow if we could do that, wouldn't we?
Melissa: Sure would.

Katie:	We'd also expand our market share in that industry, something that will further growth *and* increase profits. It's really a long-term proposition.
Melissa:	So?
Katie:	We want an A-one product, not a quick one.
Melissa:	That puts a lot of pressure on me, Katie.
Katie:	On me, too, but we have to rise to this challenge together, Melissa, or you'll always duck away from projects like this. I can't let that happen to you or to me. What you're doing contributes to this company's long-term growth and market leadership plans. And this is the first of many important accounts we'll want you to handle. Take your time—within limits—and make it good. I believe, with your talent, you have an important role to fill in this company.

Expectations

What you expect with regard to employee performance should contribute to achieving one or more of your company's business goals. We call those expectations *objectives* and *performance ranges*. They should be a part of everyone's job descriptions. They're measures of success that become the basis for coaching.

You can't improve what you can't measure, and you can't measure anything without a standard. You can't advance in a job or in a career unless you compare where you are against the benchmarks of where you want to go. Therefore, without measures and benchmarks, you can't coach someone to get to where you (and they) want them to go.

This holds true for counseling, as well. What you expect with regard to employee values and behavior should contribute to the smooth functioning of the organization in its efforts to achieve its goals. We call these expectations *behavioral standards*, and they are usually spelled out in employee handbooks. Policies and procedures are the behavioral standards by which we measure whether an employee is contributing to the smooth functioning of the organization or is getting in its way and disrupting it.

Unless the behavioral standards for your company are published, you can't expect anyone to follow them. Unless you relate what people do to those standards, you can't say that they aren't doing what you expect or ask them to change. Without behavioral standards, counseling is presumptuous at best. If your company doesn't have such a handbook, you may want to suggest it produce one.

Goals and Objectives

Goals and objectives should drive any business activity.

Katie: The team has one objective: to get the print ad campaign approved by the client by the end of the quarter. We have about a month left to create the concept, put it into words and pictures, and sell it. I gave you two weeks to test new visual ideas and to complete the artwork for two print ads—and you have all the information you need, all the talent to get the job done, and more than a week to go. You're worrying too much about only one aspect of your goal—the deadline—and that could become a tough hurdle to jump.

Katie's explanation to Melissa illustrates the nature of well-formulated goal statements (expressions of goals and objectives). Every well-formulated goal statement consists of a target, a deadline, and the conditions under which the target will be achieved (the means and resources for getting the job done and any barriers that could get in the way). Here's the skeleton of the goal statement Katie set for Melissa.

Target:	Complete the artwork for two print ads
Deadline:	Two weeks
Conditions:	Test new visual ideas
	Resources—information, talent, and time needed
	Barrier—self-induced time pressure

Katie couldn't have made the goal statement any clearer than that. Furthermore, earlier she said something to Melissa that also coached her with regard to her growth and development in the company: "We have to rise to this challenge together, Melissa, or you'll always duck away from projects like this. I can't let that happen to you or to me. What you're doing contributes to this company's long-term growth and market leadership plans. And this is the first of many important accounts we'll want you to handle. Take your time—within limits—and make it good. I believe, with your talent, you have an important role to fill in this company."

Three targets say it all: "rise to this challenge

together," "contribute to this company's long-term growth and market leadership plans," and "you have an important role to fill in this company." In a more formal coaching session, Katie can spell out more of what she means and identify the conditions that will help Melissa advance.

Performance Ranges

Expectations can excite the people you coach, or they can demotivate them. It all depends upon how you express them.

Nothing is more frustrating and demotivating than to look at a goal statement that sets one hard and fast target that may be impossible to hit. Salespeople and production workers in particular suffer from this type of rigidity: "Sell fifty units by July 31 at $500,000 each" or "Produce fifty widgets a day with no defects."

What if you sell forty-nine units by July 31 at $550,000 each? Or sell fifty-one units at $499,000 each? Have you *failed*? How about fifty-one units at $500,000 each? Are you a *superstar*? The same goes for the production worker. If you make fifty widgets a day with one defect, have you failed? How about fifty-one widgets with no defects? Are you a superstar?

Especially when you're coaching someone to improve performance, it's important to express targets as a range of possible accomplishments—*minimum acceptable, realistic expectation,* and *maximum achievable*—to make it easier for the coachee to progress up the learning curve. Taking an approach that is flexible and that takes into account levels of employee development—*recency of hire, qualitative level, balance between quality and quan-*

tity, veteran levels—leads to achieving at least minimum acceptable levels.

Recency of Hire: You can expect a new employee to perform below ordinary standards for quantity and quality of output. Some people set what they call *training standards* for new or retrained employees and expect that, by the end of the training period, the employee will reach the minimum acceptable level of production.

Qualitative Level: When you coach someone, you'll probably notice that she's very concerned with "getting it right" during the upward slope of the learning curve. Recall what one of the blindfolded people in Chapter 1 said: "Well, at least I didn't stick my fork up my nose or spill my coffee in my lap." That concern for quality usually comes at the expense of quantity; that person probably didn't eat very much. Once the quality you're looking for is mastered, you then have to coach for quantity.

Balance Between Quality and Quantity: One goal of coaching is to bring performance into balance. You have to monitor the coachee's performance to see whether he's reaching *realistic expectations*—that is, achieving the level of performance expected of any well-trained employee. A coachee's failure to achieve this balance in an expected period of time should stir you to action and generate additional coaching or training.

Veteran Level: With training and coaching, any employee should arrive at either the realistic expectations or the maximum achievable levels of performance. The goal of performance coaching is to bring everyone up to these levels. If the person you're coaching can't achieve at least realistic expectations of performance, then you may have to do some career coaching, directing the person to other positions available in the company or to positions outside the company.

Effective coaching and counseling depend on the presence of goals. You can't help people to improve performance or to grow unless they have a clear idea of where they're going, and only if there are standards will they ever know that they have arrived.

CHAPTER FOUR

How to Diagnose Actions for Change

When you're helping someone who wishes to take corrective action or to grow or stretch, you have to size up the situation and make an accurate diagnosis of the problem or the challenges. Letting nature take its course may be the worst thing you can do. The most successful changes are those you direct and manage, rather than those that you let happen.

Creating a Plan for Growth

There are many ways to help people grow and stretch in the organization. The two most common are job enrichment and career planning.

Job Enrichment: Many people become bored with their work because they reach a level at which what they're doing has become "second nature." The admission that "I can do this job in my sleep" signals a potential problem. The problem becomes more serious when the work simply can't satisfy them any more. We call this "plateauing."

You can preempt plateauing by building ways to expand a person's job or responsibilities into your planning. If you're a supervisor, take a look at your employees' job descriptions. Do they provide room for growth and development leading to higher levels of technical skill or higher levels of responsibilities? Look at what you delegate to people. Do you ask them to take on duties that you might be doing unnecessarily or to make decisions you needn't be making? Look at your work distribution pattern. Has cross-training allowed people to fill in for one another? Answers to these questions help you develop a plan for enriching people's jobs and preventing the absenteeism, tardiness, and slowdowns created by burnout.

Career Planning: Again, you can't get from here to there unless you know where there is. Successful change depends upon setting goals and designing action plans to achieve them. A weakness of some mentoring programs is that they spend a lot of time and effort coaching people to move into roles they don't want. At an international firm where I once worked, the motto was, "Train the best; keep the rest." Some of the high-priced, fast-track managers stayed in jobs they hated only because the money was good, and many of the others took the two years' training and jumped to other companies. For the vast majority of these managers, few people in charge had ever stopped to ask, "Where do you want to be in five years? What do you want to be doing? How do you want to get there?" The cost of replacing these people is high, in terms of both money and morale.

If you're coaching someone along a career path, take the time to ask questions and insist on honest answers. Identify what the person thinks she wants to achieve and compare it with what's available for her down the road.

Diagnosing a Performance Problem

A proactive person takes action before a problem becomes a crisis. It's far better to act now than to react later, when the damage may be irreversible.

Katie: I'm still not seeing the client's message here, Melissa.

Melissa: Maybe I need to use a different color combination in the foreground.

Katie: What would that accomplish?

Melissa: It would make this figure here bolder.

Katie: And what would that do?

Melissa: Hmm. You don't think that's the problem, do you?

Solving a performance problem depends upon first accurately diagnosing the problem, which requires following a five-step process:

1. Compare the actual performance with the performance standard.
2. Make an initial statement of the problem.
3. Collect data to identify causes.
4. Identify contributing factors.
5. Restate the problem.

Compare Planned and Actual Performance: The first thing you want to identify is the *planned level of performance;* that is, you need to state objectives or standards.

Katie: No, I don't, but it may be the symptom of the problem. Something's missing. I've said that before, but we won't know what it is unless we do a little diagnostic first. Melissa, what do you think our client's selling?

Melissa: Its products.

Katie: That's the physical part, but what do they want us to get across?

Melissa [*puzzled*]: I'm not sure what you're getting at.

Katie: Advertising 101, Melissa. Benefits. The "why" behind the purchase. The desired result or effect. That's what should be in this picture.

Once you've identified what that should be, the next step is to compare it with what is—with the actual performance.

Katie: What's the center of attention in your graphic?

Melissa: The product.

Make an Initial Statement of the Problem: Now you're ready to make an initial statement of the problem, which you express as an unfavorable relationship between actual and planned performance.

Katie: If the product's the center of attention, instead of the benefit, now what?

Melissa: Focus on the consumer's reaction.

Katie: That's the answer to this specific problem, but let's go beyond that to make sure that we don't have to go through this again.

Collect Data to Identify Causes: Your initial statement of the problem most likely describes symptoms, rather than the real problem. You can medicate painful symptoms all you want, but the pain will continue unless you get at what's causing it. So collect more data, and answer open-ended questions, such as these, to get beneath the surface.

- What happened?
- Where did it happen?
- How often does it happen?
- Who was involved?
- What procedures were involved?

Katie: Have you any ideas as to why you missed the benefit statement?

Melissa: Not really. I thought I understood it.

Katie: Did you use the product?

Melissa [*surprised by the question*]: No. But what if I didn't like it?

Katie: That's the risk you have to take. But you had the campaign copy, too.

Melissa: I read it.

Katie: How many times?

Melissa: Once, some of it twice.

Katie: Some of it?

Melissa: I guess I really didn't immerse myself in it, did I?

Katie: Anything like this ever happen before?

Melissa: I know what you're getting at. Is this a pattern? Especially if I'm not sure I like the product and don't believe in its benefits.

Identify Contributing Factors: Further research will help you to identify contributing factors and to understand *how* they contribute to the problem.

Melissa: I guess you're thinking that I'm a bit superficial.

Katie: No, I wasn't thinking that. I was thinking that you've let the time thing get in the way. You're not getting inside your subject. Try the product. Read and re-read the copy, then read it again. Let the consumer values surface in your own experience.

Restate the Problem: At this point, when you've uncovered as many contributing factors as you can, restate the problem, taking into account the discrepancy between planned and actual performance (i.e., the extent to which performance falls short of objectives or standards) and the consequences of not correcting the problem.

Katie: The way I see the problem is that, by focusing on your deadline, you're not focusing on your subject. The subject should be the consumer reaction—the product's benefits. But, in the interest of time, you're taking a shortcut, focusing on the product. You're 180 degrees off target and that's beginning to make your

fear of missing your deadline a possible
reality. Fortunately, we're talking about
it before the crisis stage.

Melissa: You think I should stop and start over.
Katie: That might help.

If you follow these five steps, the final statement of the problem will suggest its solution as
well.

Correcting a Behavior Problem

Solving a behavior problem requires first accurately identifying both the problem and the consequences of not changing it. To do this, you can
follow the five-step process just described, with
some variations in the content.

Compare Desired and Actual Behavior: First, collect data comparing actual performance with
what is expected according to company policies,
standards, or procedures.

Katie: Melissa, this is the third time you've left
work without telling someone.

Melissa: I'm sorry.

Katie: By now you probably know the policy
and procedures manual on this point by
heart.

Melissa: Tell someone when you're leaving early
and where you can be reached if you're
needed.

Make an Initial Statement of the Problem: Express the problem as an unfavorable relationship
between actual and expected behavior.

Katie: This is the third time in less than two
weeks you've failed to do that.

Collect Data to Identify Causes: Now you need to know more about the situation, especially why the person is violating the policy. Learning more requires collecting more data by answering more open-ended questions.

Katie: What's going on? Why does this happen?

Melissa: I'm sorry, Katie. When I'm caught up in a brainstorm, I forget everything else. I lock in on the problem, and nothing else matters.

Identify Contributing Factors: Again, you have to identify the contributing factors. How do the factors identified in the data contributed to the problem?

Katie: You simply forget.

Melissa: I'm afraid so.

Final Statement: Now, as before, express the final statement of the problem as a relationship between the contributing factors and the extent to which behavior falls short of policies, standards, or procedures.

Katie: So, as I understand the situation, you get absorbed in the problem. It fills your whole consciousness, and you simply forget everything else. That causes us a problem insofar as we have to know where you are during work hours. Things can happen fast around here, and we might need you.

Documenting Coaching or Counseling Situations

Before coaching or counseling someone about what appears to be a performance or a behavioral problem, consider why you're doing it. One instance doesn't make a problem. On the other hand, a history of mistakes or rules violations documented in a file demonstrates that a persistent and unacceptable situation exists.

Keeping an employee performance file allows you to maintain an ongoing record of all positive and negative notices of performance or behavior. Documenting situations puts you in a better position to decide when it's time to intervene. For example, a new employee needs closer supervision than an experienced employee.

Melissa is young and inexperienced, and Katie has let out the string a little longer than she would have otherwise. At the same time, you wouldn't want to come down as hard on a valued employee with an outstanding record as you would on someone whose record is spotty or suspect. In our story, Melissa has left work early without telling anyone three times. In each case, Katie has spoken with her about it and documented their conversation in the performance file.

The files should be open to employees who want to see their records, to enter notes into their files, or to respond to notes in the file. Developing such a system helps you avoid the mistake of having to "build a file" (that is, write up reports after the decision to fire or otherwise punish someone has been made).

Katie: Look, Melissa, I'm giving you a written warning—not that you shouldn't leave early, but rather that you shouldn't leave without telling someone. I'm doing it because of the number of times I've had to talk to you about this.

Melissa: I understand.

Katie: You'll need to read and sign this memo. You'll see, also, that we have a place in the memo to enter what we plan to do to correct the situation.

Melissa [*laughing*]: Tie me to the drawing board?

Katie: Nothing that drastic, I hope.

Melissa [*seriously*]: I think I've got an idea. I'm going to make a boilerplate in my computer that'll pop up every time I close a file. If I'm getting ready to leave, I'll enter date, time, reason. I can then send it to you over the LAN. If not, I'll just bypass it.

Katie: Can you program our PCs that way by yourself?

Melissa: No, but I can get Randy from Systems to help. He said I should call if ever I need him for anything.

Knowing where the coachee wants to go and can go with a job or in a career and diagnosing a problem correctly and accurately make coaching easier, more fun, and more successful. When coaching or counseling to solve a problem, the important thing is to get past the symptoms to the problem's roots. Once you do that, coaching or counseling becomes a matter of dealing with real issues, rather than with the surface of things.

CHAPTER FIVE

How to Coach Effectively

❧

Helping someone to take corrective action and guiding someone toward a desirable goal are the two most common reasons for coaching. If you're a supervisor or an experienced employee, you're doing both more than you realize.

- *Guiding someone.* Newer employees may not be creating any problems, but they usually need some kind of guidance—career path planning, networking, or just plain support. Even if your company doesn't have a consciously created mentoring program, mentoring goes on, nonetheless. When you take someone "under your wing" or just share some of your knowledge or wisdom with someone over a period of time, you're mentoring.

- *Taking corrective action.* We have to stress the importance of monitoring even trained employees. If you're the supervisor, you can do it yourself or you can ask more experienced employees to keep tabs on newer people. If you're one of those experienced employees, you can take it upon yourself to do it (if the newer employee agrees). Once you set goals and standards, you use monitoring to decide if the new hire needs additional help or is ready to learn more sophisticated or advanced methods of working. That way you prevent bad habits from creating production or quality problems. It's a proactive approach, rather than a reactive one.

How to Coach

Whatever your goal, you coach people in three different ways: in an ideal session, in an on-the-run ("curbside") session, or by modeling. Of the three ways, the ideal session seems to be the least reasonable to most people because it takes more time and resources to prepare and conduct than they believe they have. The other two occur without your even realizing it.

Ideal: The ideal coaching session is a scheduled problem-solving or planning session, with a published agenda (oral or written) and adequate time set aside. Textbooks usually prescribe about two hours. If you're teaching someone a new skill or a way to improve existing skills, you should have a lesson plan, all the resources you need, and the freedom to do what's necessary.

Most of the supervisors I've trained over the years have said the same thing: "Fat chance! When will I ever find time for this? And ask someone else to do it? When will that person have the time? And if you take an experienced person out of production, then you're losing time from two people."

Many of those supervisors are so burdened by doing everyone else's job that they rarely have time to do their own—which is to supervise. "To coach employees in need of corrective action or guidance" is a demand in the supervisory job description, but in fact most supervisors rarely have the time to do it. (To be fair, few companies rate supervisors on their coaching skills during performance appraisals, and employees are more likely to do what's demanded of them than what they can allow to slide.)

Still, to be fair to yourself as well as to employees in need of help, you should take every opportunity available to create ideal coaching sessions. The most likely times for such sessions are when a new employee is going through training, during a periodic performance review, or during a formal annual performance appraisal.

"Curbside Coaching": Few supervisors or experienced employees enjoy the luxury of having time for ideal coaching sessions. That doesn't mean that they never coach.

In reality, much coaching is "curbside," or coaching on the run. That's what Katie has been doing with Melissa. She looks at her employee's drawings and engages her in a dialogue about it; they communicate about real problems or issues related to a specific outcome. Such a conversation can take as little as a couple of minutes or as long as a couple of hours—it depends upon what has to be accomplished and how much time you have available in which to accomplish it.

Usually, the problem happens just before you coach for it. You have no time to prepare, no agenda, no lesson plan, no career ladder—nothing, just the situation to which you have to respond.

Melissa: I think I've got it. Look at these drawings, Katie.

Katie: I have just a couple of minutes before going to a meeting, but let's take a look. Hmm. Interesting work. I like this one; it's really saying something to me. That other one—I don't know. What are you trying to say?

Melissa: This product'll make your life more enjoyable. You can't see that, huh?

Katie: Maybe, but that's kind of generic, isn't it? Wouldn't any other similar product make your life more enjoyable?

Melissa: Yeah. I see your point. But I'm glad you like the one.

Katie: It's great. See what you can do about the second one to bring home the message, and I'll talk with you about it later.

Forty-five seconds—including time to look at the drawings. And in those scant seconds, Katie and Melissa included all four steps of effective coaching.

The Four-Step Method

In ideal and ''curbside'' coaching, a four-step method facilitates the process. How you use this

Four-Step Method of Effective Coaching

1. Openers
2. The exchange (getting and giving information)
3. Resolving differences
4. Designing an action plan

method can encourage or discourage the employee being coached.

Openers: Melissa produced the opener by dashing into Katie's office with her drawings, but Katie followed through by taking the few seconds to look at the drawings. (Had she been actually walking out the door, she could have handled it just as well by saying something like, "I'm heading out to an important meeting. Walk with me. I'll look at the pictures, and we can get together when I get back.")

Under more propitious circumstances, you can set the stage for a coaching session by (1) setting the employee at ease with a warm and friendly manner, (2) identifying the purpose of the meeting, (3) reviewing the meeting's agenda (if you have one), and (4) getting the employee's commitment to looking at the situation (such as a performance problem or a career move) and taking the necessary steps. Now, you're ready to move on.

Particularly when a problem is involved, the openers are extremely important. The atmosphere you create will determine whether you can get anywhere.

Katie: Thanks for stopping what you're doing to come in. Have a seat.

Melissa: A problem?

Katie: Nothing we can't work out. You know I'm pleased with your efforts on this project. Only one thing concerns me—the way in which you've approached it. But I think it's a simple matter of organization.

Melissa: I don't understand.

Katie: Look. To clarify my issues, here's what I'd like to do. First, let's look at how you attacked the project; you tell me the steps you've taken to get it started. Then I'll tell you what I'm thinking, and if we have any issues around your process, we can resolve them. I think we can come up with a way of getting you on target faster and without as much supervision. That way, you can take on more responsibilities on your own—which will help you with your own career. Okay?

Melissa: Sure.

All the keys to an effective opening are here, yet it took only a few seconds to lay them out. Most important, Katie showed Melissa the benefit to *her* of doing what has to be done: the opportunity to advance her career.

The Exchange: While telling Melissa what she wants to talk about, Katie has also asked the employee to describe how she sets about attacking a project—the steps she takes. She's *getting information.* It's essential to the coach to know what the coachee thinks and feels before launching into *giving information.* To do otherwise is merely to lecture, or worse.

By getting information, you also find out what obstacles you might have to manage if the person doesn't agree with you that a problem exists or if he feels angry or bad about the situation.

Melissa [*summing up her position*]: I know I didn't really get into the subject deeply enough at first, but even though it took me a little more time, I finally did get fully into it.

Katie: You think I'm asking for too much.

Melissa: Well, I'm feeling uncomfortable with this conversation. Like you think I don't know what I'm doing.

Katie: That's really not my point. I think you're extremely talented. On the other hand, I think you can make more of that talent than you're doing. I'd like to give you some feedback about your process that could help you in the long run. Is that okay with you?

Now, Katie can express her opinions.

Resolving Differences: The whole purpose of the exchange is to surface differences, but if you let those differences just lie on the table without doing anything about them, they won't go away. Instead, they'll skulk around until they have an opportunity to bite someone—usually you.

Katie: Do you see what I mean about not picking up a pencil until after you've examined everything about the subject?

Melissa: Not really. It seems like it'll take more time, not less.

Katie: You know how you get up and walk out when you're in a brainstorm?

Melissa: Yes.

Katie: What are you doing when you do that?

Melissa: I go for a walk. Let the storm clear.

Katie: I think we can prevent the storms. It's like an egg hatching. I'm recommending that you incubate ideas at the front end rather than run into storms later. I think you'll find fewer storms in your way.

Melissa: It's worth a try.

Katie: I think so. Let's talk about how to do it.

Now they're ready for the last step.

Action Planning: Once you've resolved your differences, together you can plan what to do to correct a problem, to take another career step, or to accomplish whatever your meeting is designed to accomplish.

Modeling

Most coaching is not done through formal and informal sessions such as we've been describing. Most of it is done by modeling, or coaching through behavior.

You teach people what you expect from them by setting expectations without realizing it through what you say and do. People watch you to see what you're like, what you will accept and won't accept. They also watch to see what you do in order to emulate what they see; they become "clones" (to the best of their ability) because they realize that you will reward behavior that you approve of, and what you do, you usually approve of. (Yes, there are the "do-as-I-say-not-as-I-do" exceptions.)

In short, you teach people how to relate to you by how you relate to them. You teach people what to do by doing the same things yourself.

Coaching people effectively produces the results you're looking for. Using the four-step method creates change. At the same time, it reinforces the coachee's self-esteem because it isn't accusatory or punitive. But you have to plan the changes in appropriate increments in order not to overwhelm people with impossible demands.

You also have to provide the person being coached with opportunities for small successes.

By recognizing incremental gains, you reward the coachee's efforts and provide positive reinforcement. Just succeeding is rewarding, and, as the saying goes, small successes do breed big ones.

CHAPTER SIX

How to Counsel Effectively

∽

To avoid confusion, we've deliberately limited the word *counseling* to mean taking corrective action to change behavior. That's because the word seems to carry a negative connotation. You go for counseling to resolve marital conflicts, or to get your life straightened out, or to find a vocation or a career for yourself. So, too, at work. You get counseling when you've messed up—the way Melissa did by not telling anyone that she was leaving work early.

When to Counsel

In Chapter Four I asked you to guard against acting too precipitously. One instance of a behavior does not make a problem. I've also said that people can't meet your expectations if they don't know what you expect of them. That requires a proper orientation as to the expectations and monitoring appropriate to the environment and to the people involved.

Orientation

Many companies don't have an orientation program. They may tell new employees about benefits or issue a published handbook and tell the new people to read it; a small handful review key points, such as hours of work and policies on absence. Common reasons for not having an orientation are, "We don't have time" and, "They're adults. They ought to know what's expected of them when they come to work." A look at the turnover rates at these companies might be instructive.

First impressions are important. Studies have shown that the first three days on the job make the most lasting impressions on the employee. That's when new people learn the real terms and conditions of the *psychological contract* that implicitly exists between themselves and their employers. That's when they learn the rules and agree to abide by them. That's when they learn what the employers expect of them and what they can expect from their employers. Many a letdown has occurred at this early point in the employee's career.

From the employer's point of view, orientation is the time to define the organization's values, set limits for acceptable behavior, and model the behavior expected from employees. An effective orientation opens two-way channels of communication, describes the organization's culture, and establishes the atmosphere in which employees work. The more open and honest the employer is, the more positive will be the employees' responses to the organization.

The orientation does one more thing. It sets the standards by which you as a supervisor can judge people's behavior. If you tell workers that using illegal drugs or drinking alcohol on the job (including working meals) is unacceptable and they agree (by signing a form to that effect or by other means), you have a basis for discharging them if you find them violating the rules; if you don't tell them, they can sue you for taking punitive action against them. If your company doesn't have a formal orientation program, you can take the initiative and do the orienting yourself.

Monitoring: You have to decide for yourself what to monitor, when to monitor, and how to monitor. How strict or how lax you choose to be will depend upon the work involved, the quality of the people hired, the quality of the supervisors, and the quality of the orientation. Highly motivated people excited by their work, loyal to their companies, and satisfied by the kind of supervision they get need little or no monitoring. Melissa doesn't intend to break the rules; she becomes absent-minded when locked in her "brainstorms." Katie's reactions are relatively mild, the written warning being required by company rules.

In most cases, monitoring helps you manage real issues. And you don't have to be a supervisor to do this, either. Although it's not her place to counsel Melissa, Rose, the department's secretary, can alert Melissa to the violation of a rule.

Rose: Melissa? You leaving?
Melissa: Yeah. I've got a problem I'm trying to work out. Got to walk around and think about it.

Rose: Did you tell Katie? You know the rules.

Melissa: Oh, gee. I forgot. Have a pad of paper handy? [*writing*] Put this in her mail box for me, will you? Thanks.

A more experienced employee might also counsel her.

Randy: Okay. Let me get this straight. You forget to let Katie know you're leaving when you leave early.

Melissa: Yep.

Randy: That can cause you big problems. Things break around here pretty fast.

Melissa: I know that, but what do you think I can do? I don't mean to break the rules; I just get caught up in my own head and forget.

Randy: Your idea of a boilerplate in the LAN is a good one. We should all have one, I guess, but it's not a big issue for anyone else. I think we can make one for you that'll work, as long as you don't forget to use it. Here's what you'll have to do. Make sure you close your file anytime you leave your computer. Even if it's just to go to the rest room. Your boilerplate will pop up, and it'll ask you to enter date, time, and reason for leaving your file. If you're leaving the area, hit enter when it asks you if you want to send the message to Rose and to Katie. What do you think?

The key to the successful peer counseling here is that Melissa came to Randy. Most people resent unsolicited advice. Sometimes, even asking, "May I give you a piece of advice?" can evoke an unceremonious "No" and a great deal of anger.

What Makes Counseling Work

Giving feedback and helping a person manage a behavioral problem take planning and careful handling.

Feedback: The word *feedback* refers to information you provide people on how their behavior affects you. It can also signify, in some way, that a goal or standard has been or has not been achieved. *Informational feedback* refers to the verification of information with another person to ensure you understand one another or the comparison of what is with what should be. *Behavioral feedback* refers to letting people know how their behavior affects you as well as how you feel about it.

You give feedback most effectively:

- Where there is a climate of trust and caring
- When it is sought by the recipient
- If the recipient's as well as your needs are met
- If the feedback is accepted nondefensively
- If, before giving feedback, you test the accuracy of your perceptions
- If feedback is expressed in terms of what you perceive, feel, and need and each element is expressed separately and clearly

Informational Feedback. You can focus informational feedback in the following ways:

- Compare actual performance with an objective plan or standard.
- Give feedback with respect to something said by paraphrasing or restating the origi-

nal statement, rather than by repeating it verbatim (parroting).

- State feedback in terms of what you believe the other person said ("If I understand you, I have to give notice if I'm leaving early").
- Use nonverbal feedback (a physical action) only to show that you understand instructions on how to do something by actually performing the task.
- Check feedback for accuracy.

Behavioral Feedback. You can focus behavioral feedback in the following ways:

- Describe behaviors over which the recipient has some control, rather than perceived personality traits.
- Focus feedback on direct and relatively recent experiences, not on inferences or hearsay.
- Be specific as well as descriptive.
- Explain how the behavior affects you or the performance of a task for which you are ultimately responsible, and explain the consequences, as you see them, if the adverse behavior continues.
- Mix negative and positive feedback appropriately to give support without withdrawing the negative feedback.
- Avoid sticking negative feedback between two positive statements ("prickly sandwich").
- Allow the recipient to choose from among several options for changing or not changing behavior.
- Exchange information and share ideas, rather than making feedback a one-way communication.

- Ask for feedback about your feedback.

Let's look at things Katie says that reflect these guidelines and that lead to Melissa's having Randy put the boilerplate into the computer.

Katie: Okay, let me summarize. You left work yesterday without telling me again. You know I think you're doing good work. The only thing that bothers me is your leaving work early without letting me know. I have to know where you are if we need you. This written warning says that your failure to change this behavior will affect your performance appraisal with respect to reliability. Now, you can do nothing about it and hope for the best. You can make a conscious change. Or you can let me make the decisions, which I would rather not do.

Melissa: No. As I said, I'll make the change myself.

Katie: Which is?

Melissa: I'll get Randy to help me set up a message board for us.

The Counseling Session: A proper counseling session implies: (1) a scheduled problem-solving or planning meeting, (2) a published agenda (oral or written), and (3) adequate time set aside to resolve the problem. All this notifies the other person that it's a serious matter about which you feel strongly enough to set other matters aside and that you've given the matter a great deal of thought. This way you model the behavior you expect. Again, you don't have to be a supervisor to follow these steps; anyone can counsel another person as long as it's appropriate to do so.

The four-step method that we reviewed in Chapter 5 facilitates the process. The openers are very important, because when you're dealing with a major issue, such as a rules violation, the other person must be receptive to what you're saying. What do you think Katie would have accomplished by saying, "Melissa, you're a lazy shirker. Leave work early again, and you're fired!"?

Unless you get information from the other person during the exchange, you won't know with what you're dealing, and won't be able to make effective decisions. Unless you resolve differences of opinions or values, your decisions will be hollow and doomed to failure. And unless you design an action plan around mutually acceptable decisions, you'll be wasting both your and the other person's time.

Don't make the counseling session an all-or-nothing proposition. Asking for behavioral changes takes time; people don't change their ways of doing things overnight. Counseling takes as much patience as does coaching, maybe more. Often the issues are value-laden and emotional. In addition, the changes you're planning together involve resistant behavior patterns, rather than performance skills. So plan the counseling process in appropriate increments.

If you're a supervisor providing counseling, be sure the person being counseled receives verbal warnings and is given sufficient time to change the behavior. Explain the consequences of changing and not changing behavior. Record the verbal warnings in the employee's file. If necessary, provide the person being counseled with a written warning and with additional time for changing behavior. Have the employee acknowledge receipt of the warning and add comments, if desired. And be sure to reward positive results by offering at least recognition.

Katie: I think your system's going to work. I received your message board in my PC yesterday. Thanks.

Since entering into a counseling relationship is a major undertaking, you shouldn't begin one lightly. If you do find yourself in this role, be patient, be supportive, give effective, useful feedback, and let the other person make the decisions and the plans necessary for making changes. The whole process can then be rewarding for everyone.

Conclusion

"[My coach] really helped me a lot. He was very caring but didn't do everything for me. He just saw to it that I did everything I had to do." That's what effective coaches and counselors do—they help other people do what they have to do. They help people *renew* themselves or *redirect* what they are doing or how they are doing it. From a short-term perspective, coaching may seem to be a waste of resources, both yours and the organization's, but in the long term it pays off in more productive people and in the growth of the work group of which you are a part.

Breaking through the short-term perspective to the longer view requires learning another way of looking at what people are doing and how they do it, and especially at how they meet challenges requiring new and creative thinking. Rather than telling people what to do and how to do it, effective coaching consists of helping people learn *how to learn*—how to diagnose and solve problems, how to identify new paths for their own growth and development, and how to help the organization do the same.

To coach and counsel people most effectively, you must let them learn through your guidance and your modeling. Use the five steps suggested for diagnosing problems to help people learn how to solve their own problems and to make decisions for themselves. Use the four-step method for conducting coaching or counseling sessions to help people open themselves up to new ways of doing their work more effectively or to new ways to grow. Both approaches will help you help other people help themselves—the way the blindfolded people learned to feed themselves.

Suggested Readings

❧

Herzberg, Frederick. "One More Time: How Do You Motivate Employees? Not By Improving Work Conditions, Raising Salaries, or Shuffling Tasks." In *People: Managing Your Most Important Asset*. Boston: Harvard Business Review, 1990.

————. *Work and the Nature of Man.* New York: New American Library, 1973.

Lawrence, Paul R. "How to Deal With Resistance to Change." In *People: Managing Your Most Important Asset.* Boston: Harvard Business Review, 1990.

Mager, Peter E., and Peter Pipe. *Analyzing Performance Problems, or ''You Really Oughta Wanna.''* Belmont, Calif.: Fearon Publishing/Lear Siegler, 1970.

Mehrabian, Albert. *Nonverbal Communication.* Chicago: Aldine, 1972.

Melohn, Thomas H. "How to Build Employee Trust and Productivity." In *People: Managing Your Most Important Asset.* Boston: Harvard Business Review, 1990.

Sherman, V. Clayton. *From Losers to Winners: Managing Problem Employees.* New York: AMACOM, 1987.

Skinner, B. F. *Beyond Freedom and Dignity.* New York: Knopf, 1971.

Weiss, Donald H. *How to Deal With Difficult People.* New York: AMACOM, 1987.

————. *How to Delegate Effectively.* New York: AMACOM, 1988.

————. *How to Get the Best Out of People.* New York: AMACOM, 1988.

Index

✧

About the Author

Donald H. Weiss, Ph.D., is CEO of Self-Management Communications, Inc., St. Louis, and a well-known author of books, videos, and cassette-workbook programs that focus on management and interpersonal skills. He has been a senior training and development executive and consultant for more than twenty-five years. Among his corporate positions were: program manager for the Citicorp Executive Development Center and corporate training manager for Millers' Mutual Insurance. His many publications include fifteen previous books in the SOS series and *Fair, Square, and Legal: Safe Hiring, Managing, and Firing Practices to Keep Your Company Out of Court* (all AMACOM). Dr. Weiss earned his Ph.D. from Tulane University.